Contents

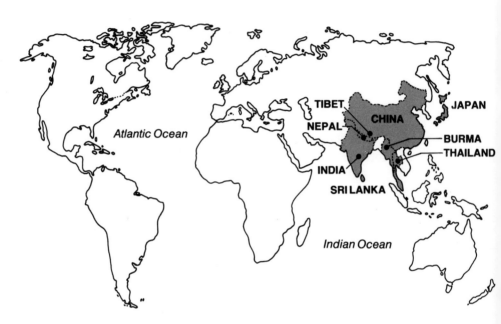

Buddhist countries of Asia.

Chris Hardy

BUDDHA

Series Editor: Ray Bruce

 Holt, Rinehart and Winston Ltd

Cover illustration: Illustration acknowledgements
Head of Buddha
*The publishers would like to thank the following for permission to use
their material: Barnaby's Picture Library for pp. 15, 22, 23, 33, 43, 46, 50,
51, 58, 59, 62, 63 and the cover photograph; John Claxton for pp. 8, 9, 26,
30, 31, and 34; Phaidon Press for pp. 12, 13, 16, 17, 20, 24, 25, 28, 32, 40
and 56.*

Holt, Rinehart and Winston Ltd
1 St Anne's Road,
Eastbourne, East Sussex BN21 3UN

ISBN 0 03 910449 4

Designed and typeset by DP Press, Sevenoaks, Kent.
Maps by Daphne Fleetwood
Printed in Great Britain by Cambus Litho, East Kilbride.
Colour reproduction by Anglia Reproductions.

Print Number 987654321

1 India, 563 BCE

Siddhartha Gautama was born in the small city of Kapilavattu, on the border between the countries we now call India and Nepal. When he was a grown man he used to tell people, 'There is a country close to a slope of the Himalayas. Its people are rich and brave. They are descended from the Sun and are called Sakyas, from that family have I gone forth.'

The name Siddhartha means, 'He whose aim is achieved', and was his 'first' name. Gautama was his clan or family name, what we might call his surname. He was a prince of the Sakya tribe of warriors. His father Shuddhodana was the Rajah, or king, of the tribe and his mother's name was Maya.

It is thought that Gautama was born in about 563 BCE and died eighty years later in 483 BCE. He spent his entire life wandering in a fairly small area of India which the people called 'The Middle Country'.

Many hundreds of years before a whole race of people calling themselves Aryans had invaded India and enslaved the people living there. The Aryans worshipped gods similar to those of the Ancient Greeks (their god Dyaus was the same as the Greek Zeus). They organized their *society* very carefully, by dividing the people in it into groups called Varnas (which means 'colours'). The modern word for Varna, used in India and elsewhere today, is caste. The most important and powerful group was the Brahmin Varna. The Brahmins were priests. They had control over the Aryan religion because only they could use the *sacred books*, the Vedas. In these books were hymns, spells, chants and instructions on how to contact and influence the gods.

The next Varna down the scale was that of the warriors, the Kshatriyas. The third Varna was that of the Vaisyas, the merchants and farmers. But all of the members of these Varnas were Aryans and the local Indian people were not allowed into this *privileged* world. They were expected just to work for the Aryans. Gautama's tribe, the Sakyas, may have been Kshatriyas or they may have been hill people from the Himalayas like today's Tibetans and Nepalese, and not Aryans at all.

The people of India who were not allowed into the Varna system naturally disliked this way of ordering life. They had an ancient society of their own and many *religious ideas and*

5

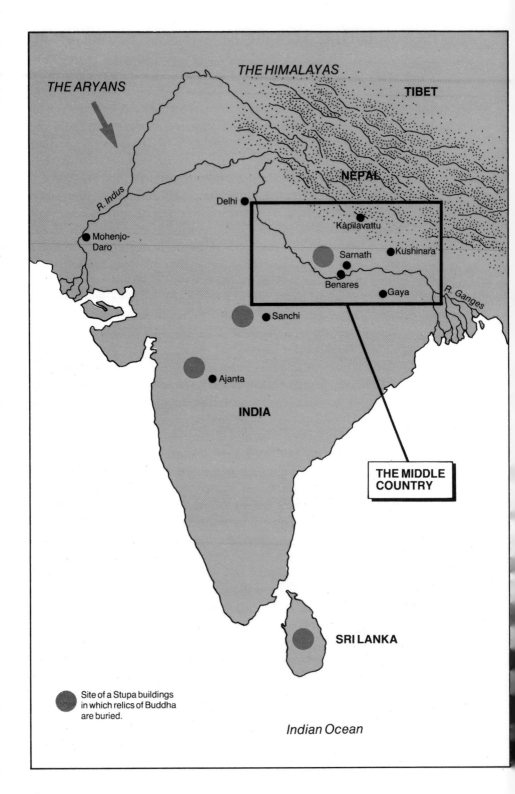

THE ARYANS

THE HIMALAYAS

TIBET

NEPAL

R. Indus

Delhi

Kapilavattu

Mohenjo-
Daro

Sarnath

Kushinara

Benares

Gaya

R. Ganges

Sanchi

THE MIDDLE
COUNTRY

Ajanta

INDIA

SRI LANKA

Site of a Stupa buildings
in which relics of Buddha
are buried.

Indian Ocean

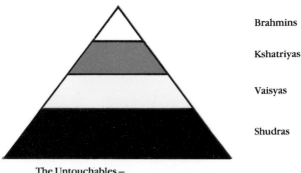

Brahmins

Kshatriyas

Vaisyas

Shudras

The *Varna* or Caste System.

The Untouchables – Outside the Caste System – Outcasts

◁A map of India 563 B.C.E.

Over page: Two Indian 'Saddhus', who live homeless lives, without jobs or money, spending their days thinking and teaching about their religious beliefs. As in Buddha's time the people feed these wanderers, and welcome them to their villages.

practices, but these were scorned by the Brahmins. The Indian people wanted to be able to have pride in their religion and to be respected and accepted in the new Indian society, but the Brahmins would not allow it. Also they demanded that very expensive *sacrifices* be made to the gods, which most of the ordinary Indian people could not afford.

Other people disliked the Brahmins and their Vedic religion too. Many Aryans, especially among the Kshatriyas, thought the spells, chants and sacrifices were a waste of time. This kind of religion did not answer the questions about life which people ask and expect religion to answer, such as, 'Why are we here in the *Universe*?' or, 'Where do we go when we die?' or, 'What is real happiness and how do you get it?' Some Aryan *philosophers* thought out a new way of explaining these and other mysteries, which they wrote down in poems called Upanishads. Unfortunately, these ideas were very hard to understand and were of no more help to most people in their efforts to make sense of their lives and find some sort of lasting happiness than were those of the Brahmins.

So in the society to which Gautama belonged there was much quarrelling and discussing. It was into this atmosphere that he was born. We can read how, when he was older, he argued with Brahmins and Aryan philosophers about the things they believed and did. But other people were wandering around India searching for answers to life's problems. These wandering holy men and thinkers were part of life in India before the Aryans came and they are still found all over India today. Gautama argued with them too: the Saddhus, wandering holy men who practised forms of what we call Yoga; the Jains, who believed in *non-violence* and *reincarnation*; *Atheists*; and others.

7

But this was when Gautama had found what he thought was the truth, and was preaching it. This was when he had already become 'The Buddha', which means the *enlightened* one'. (The word 'enlightened' means suddenly seeing the truth. To be enlightened is to be like someone trapped in a pitch-black room for days. Suddenly the door is opened, light floods in and the way out is clear.) 'Buddha' is not a name, but a *title*, in the same way that 'Christ' is not a name but a title of Jesus. Gautama also used to call himself a 'Tathagata', which means 'One who has gone', or 'One who is free'. But before he earned these titles and became 'Sakya Muni', or Wise-Man of the Sakyas, he lived the life of a Prince in the Palace of Kapilavattu.

Things to do

1. Find out what the words in italics mean in Chapter 1. Make a special section in your workbook for these words. Write them down with their meanings. You will be asked to add to the list as you go on through this book.
2. Copy the map or draw your own.
3. The Brahmins did eventually allow another Varna to be added to the first three. This was the Shudra Varna and was for labourers and craftsmen, many of whom were not Aryans. But many people were still left outside the Varna or caste system (as it is called today). These were the 'Outcasts' or 'Untouchables'. There are millions of these people in India even today.

    (a) What do the words 'outcast' and 'untouchable' mean?
    (b) Do we have anything like a caste system in our society today?
    (c) Do we have any Outcasts or Untouchables?
4. Make a list of the mysteries of life which you would like answers to.
5. Find out what you can about the gods and goddesses of Ancient Greece.
6. What do BCE and CE mean? Draw a line on your page, either vertical or horizontal. Then make a mark in the middle of it and label it '0'. Then mark on your diagram the birth dates of some of the people who began religions.
7. Look carefully at the diagram of the Varna system. Do the colours mean anything to you?

2 Gautama's Early Life

The story of Gautama's birth sounds strange to us, but so does the story of Jesus' birth to many people! For *Buddhists* and *Christians*, the most important thing about these stories is not so much what they say as what they really mean. What are they trying to tell us? Both stories try to show that here we have the arrival in the world of a *unique* person.

Winter was past and the first month of Spring had come, all the flowers and trees were in blossom and the weather was mild, neither too hot nor too cold. The Buddha, living in *Heaven*, made ready to enter the womb of Queen Maya, wife of Rajah Shuddhodana in the kingdom of Kapilavattu.

That night as she slept the Buddha came down and entered her womb. As he did so she had a wonderful dream. She saw a six-tusked elephant with a head the colour of rubies coming out of the heavens and entering her right side. When morning came she told the king of her dream. He sent for eight Brahmins, who could *interpret dreams*. They told the king that the dream was a *good omen*, for it meant that the queen was pregnant and her child would gain perfect *wisdom*.

Time passed and Maya felt the hour of birth was close. Her father sent messengers to Shuddhodana saying that he was afraid that his daughter would die when the child was born. He asked if she could come and rest in his house. So Queen Maya, with her musicians, dancing women and guards, set out on the journey. When they reached the gardens near her father's home she stepped down from her chariot and walked beneath the shade of a sala tree. She took hold of a branch and looked up into the heavens.

Seeing his mother Maya standing like this the Buddha arose and was born from her right side as she was standing under the tree. Then, without any help, he walked seven steps towards each quarter of the horizon. At every step a lotus flower sprang from the earth beneath his feet. He then said, 'This is my last body, I shall have no more lives to endure. I shall wipe out the sorrow that is caused by birth and death.'

The belief that all living beings live many lives, known as 'reincarnation', has always been a part of the religions of India. Buddhists and Hindus believe in it and Buddhists believe that Gautama lived many thousands of lives before his final one

The miraculous birth of the Buddha. Compare this story with some of the Greek myths about the birth of the gods and goddesses. Also note that the baby seems to have a sort of halo, as the baby Jesus does in many Christian works of art.

Asita and the wise men in the garden at Suddhodana's palace, advising the king on his son's future. Look at the way one of them is sitting in the 'Lotus' position. People who practise yoga still meditate sitting this way. Asita himself seems to have been fasting (see the beginning of Chapter 3). This carving comes from a large Buddhist temple in Java. This shows how Buddhism spread. How far is Java from India?

The young prince Siddhartha and the harem his father is said to have provided for him. The prince is wearing the sacred thread which shows that he has passed from boyhood to manhood. Hindu boys still go through the 'Sacred Thread' ritual today.

(which is the subject of our story). In India today the rituals which celebrate the birth of a child begin before the child is born because Hindus believe the soul of the baby arrives in its body before it is born. Once the birth has taken place then *astrologers* are called to the house, and this happened when the baby Siddhartha Gautama was born too. The astrologers who came to the palace *predicted* many things but none said that the baby would be an ordinary prince. The wise old man, Asita, with tangled hair, seeing Gautama on the yellow blanket like a coin of gold beneath the white sunshade, was overjoyed. He told the Sakyas, 'This boy will reach the summit of enlightenment' and he wept because he knew he would not be there to see it, or learn the truth from the Buddha.

Asita and the other astrologers said that Gautama would leave home to become a wandering holy man. Shuddhodana, already saddened by the death of Queen Maya soon after his son's birth, was made even more unhappy by this *prophecy*. He decided to keep Gautama safe and secure in the palace and its large grounds, surrounded by luxury and friends, and unaware of life in the world outside.

LIFE IN THE PALACE From Buddhist stories and what we know of how other Indian princes lived we can work out what Gautama's youth might have been like.

His room in the palace had a soft bed with a finely decorated canopy over it. There were two pillows, one at each end of the bed. Near the verandah leading out into the garden was a chair and a small table with fresh flowers on it. On another table were drawing materials, some books and a board for chess. His clothes and other belongings were kept in large chests made of hard, brown teak. By his window the king had had an aviary built, full of colourful, tuneful birds. There were swings and a fountain in the garden, too, and shaded grass banks where Siddhartha could sit and talk with friends.

Early every morning, he would have a bath and then rub perfumed oils into his skin. After cleaning his teeth with a twig he would put on black eye make-up and a sort of lipstick. All these things were usual for wealthy men, as well as for women. Then he would put on a fresh robe, his golden earrings and bracelets and wait for a servant to bring breakfast. This was bread, milk and juicy tropical fruit: pineapples, mangoes and sometimes grapes.

After breakfast his friends, the sons of courtiers, came to see him and they played the sort of games that boys have always

A Hindu bride of today. Yasodhara would have dressed in similar, if not richer, finery.

played. But everyday Siddhartha would have to leave his friends for a few hours, to go and study with his Brahmin *Guru*, or teacher. He learnt about the gods and how the universe was ordered by them. He learnt about the duties of a Brahmin, and a king. He learnt how to read and write, and perhaps how to paint and play the sitar.

Because he was a prince and a warrior Siddhartha also learned how to fight. A captain from his father's army showed him how to use a sword and a dagger, a spear and a bow and arrow. He learned how to use these weapons on foot and on horseback. Buddhist stories tell us that he was the best young horseman and archer at the court.

So time went by. The Prince grew up in the beautiful, peaceful palace at Kapilavattu, earning the friendship and respect of all who knew him, not knowing how different life was for most people beyond the walls of the palace grounds. As he got older his father made sure that he met plenty of girls but, when he was nineteen, the time came for his marriage to be arranged. (It is still the custom in India and some other places for marriages to be arranged by the parents of the

15

couple.) A beautiful girl called Yasodhara, the daughter of a minister at the court, was thought to be the best choice. But, and this is still the custom too, the couple had the right to meet and then say 'No', if they so wished. Yasodhara met Siddhartha at a contest between princes. As usual Siddhartha beat the others at riding and archery. Soon after they were married and within a year Yasodhara gave birth to a son, Rahula. Many years of marriage followed, the young family living happily in their own fine rooms in the palace.

LEAVING HOME

Gautama naturally became restless to find out more about life as it really was in the world outside. He tried to get his friend and charioteer Chandra to take him out. When his father heard of his son's plans he made up his mind to let him go. But he gave orders that anyone who was ill or deformed or very poor should be kept away from the road because he did not want his son to see them. So all the cripples, the old, the mad and the beggars were driven away.

As the Prince was driven into the town the people cheered. Gautama saw, for the first time, the houses and shops and streets of ordinary people. The Buddhist story of his visit goes on like this:

16

A Burmese statue of the prince cutting off his hair. Notice how the face of Buddha differs from picture to picture. Why do you think this is?

'The Gods of the Pure Abode, when they saw that everyone was happy as if in *Paradise*, conjured up the image of an old man. The Prince's charioteer told him about old age. The Prince reacted to this news like a bull when lightning crashes down near him. He said to Chandra, "So that is how old age destroys the memory, beauty and strength of all. And yet with such a sight before it the world goes on quite undisturbed!" The Prince then asked to be driven back to the palace.

'On his second journey into the town he saw a man crippled by disease. On his third journey he saw a dead body being carried to the burning ground. Leaning over the chariot rail he called out, "This is the end that has been fixed for all and yet the world takes no notice! Turn back the chariot! This is no time for pleasure, how can anyone pay no attention when he knows of his approaching end?"

'On his fourth visit he met a wandering holy man, a Saddhu, who owned nothing but a robe and a begging bowl. The Prince told Chandra to stop the chariot and spoke to the man, "Honoured Sir, tell me what sort of a man you are". He answered, "I am one who has left the world and its ways, my home and friends, so as to find *salvation* and do good. I am called a homeless one". Siddhartha asked him more questions and then got down from the chariot and walked three times round the Saddhu as a sign of respect. He then returned with Chandra to the palace.'

As a result of these experiences Gautama began to ask the kind of questions which people often ask themselves, but which had never bothered him before: 'What is the point of life if we are all going to die anyway?' 'How can we face life when we know there is so much suffering going on?' 'How is it that we can forget how others suffer?' 'How can we find out, and get rid of, the causes of suffering?' But unlike most people, Gautama decided to do something to find the answers to these questions.

The things he had seen in Kapilavattu had such a powerful effect on him that he found his whole life was changed: all the things which had once been important were now not at all important. Things, which he had never heard of before became the only things he thought about. We call this total change in a person's feelings and thoughts a *religious experience*, because, very suddenly, a person who has a religious experience will go from leading a normal life to one given over completely to the religious way of life and the search for the truth. Like Gautama, Jesus and Muhammad also had religious experiences which changed their lives; Jesus at his baptism and Muhammad in a cave in the desert.

Late one night Gautama whispered goodbye to his sleeping wife and son and rode off to the jungle with Chandra. On the edge of the forest he gave all he had to his friend, including his beloved horse Kanthaka, and he cut off the long hair of a prince. Taking off his fine clothes he put on a simple orange robe and, picking up his begging bowl, said goodbye to his friend and went off alone into the dark forest. Remembering these moments later Gautama was to say that home was, 'A place of dust' and leaving it was like, 'Going into the open air'. 'While still a black-haired youth, while my parents wept, I cut off my hair and putting on a yellow robe went from a home to a houseless life.'

NOTES
1. It has always been accepted in India that some people are destined to leave their homes and become wandering holy men. This does not mean to say that their families are always pleased when it happens!

2. Gautama's leaving home is called by Buddhists the 'Great Renunciation' because he renounced, or gave up entirely, his previous way of life and went out to find a new and better one.

Things to do

1. Find out what the words in italics mean in Chapter 2.
2. What is astrology? Why do you think some people want to know about their future? Do you?
3. How can we tell from the story of Gautama's birth that Buddhists believe in reincarnation?
4. The Buddhist story says that it was the gods who conjured up the things Gautama saw in the town. How else can we explain what he saw?
5. Why did seeing these things have such a powerful effect on the prince? Why did his father not want him to see anything like that, do you think?
6. What do you think impressed Gautama most about the holy man?
7. Gautama gave up everything he had and was left with almost nothing. What would you have to leave behind to end up like him?
8. Put yourself in the prince's place. Write the story we have read in Chapter 2 from his point of view, *or*, make a comic strip of the story we have read in Chapter 2.
9. What do you think Gautama meant by his remarks about his home and about leaving it, near the end of Chapter 2?

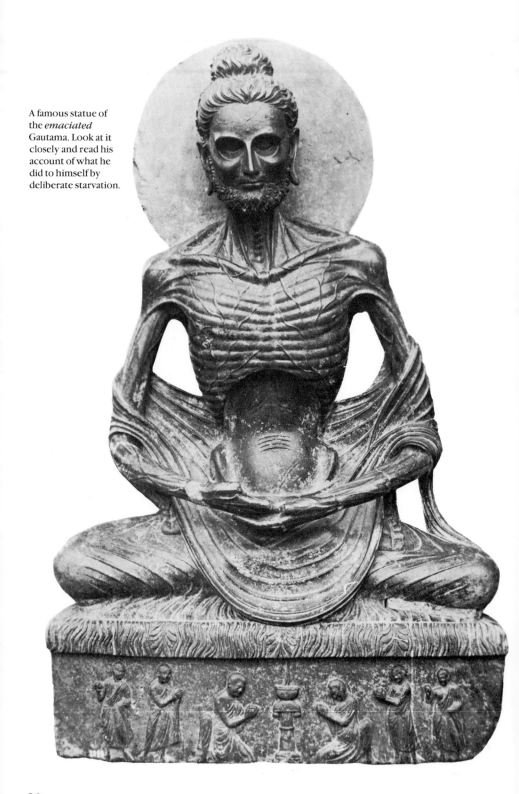

A famous statue of the *emaciated* Gautama. Look at it closely and read his account of what he did to himself by deliberate starvation.

3 The Search for Enlightenment

THE SEARCH Siddhartha wandered about the vast, flat, empty countryside of the north Indian plain looking for help in answering the questions which had begun to bother him after his religious experience in the streets of Kapilavattu. At first he stayed with two Brahmins but their ideas were of no use to him.

Then on a hot summer's day he came to a place called Nairanjana. The country was wild and rocky with many caves. It was still and silent. Nearby was a great river, but no fishermen. The river was so huge it seemed at least seven miles wide. On its banks and in the caves, and out in the burning heat, Saddhus were practising *Yoga*. As Siddhartha walked towards them he felt strange, he was still not used to wearing just a single robe and being without servants and friends and his horse. He explained to a group of five of the holy men all that had happened to him. He asked for their help.

The Saddhus believed that human beings had a *soul*, called 'Atman'. This soul was a part of the Universal Soul, called 'Brahman'. 'Brahman' is not a god but a power, the power which keeps the universe alive. The Saddhus believed that all human suffering was caused by the separation of the Atman from the Brahman. They also believed that the only way to re-unite the two was by getting complete control over their bodies and minds. This involved training themselves to endure great physical hardship.

Because he too wanted to find out what was the real cause of human suffering Gautama joined with them in their *ascetic* life. Later he described what it was like: the Saddhus tried all sorts of things to test if they had mastered their bodies; they might stand on one leg for days, or sit by a fire staring up into the sun. Gautama tried holding his breath, which caused a pain, 'As if a butcher was cutting my head with a sharp knife.' For six years he starved himself:

> 'My body became extremely lean. My limbs were like thin plants with black joints. The mark of my seat was like a camel's footprint and my ribs stuck out like the beams of an old shed. My skin was cracked and withered and my eyes sparkled like the water in the bottom of a deep well. When I touched my stomach I actually got hold of my spine! And yet I did not attain true knowledge.'

*Above:*The flat, hot plains of northern India over which Buddha would have wandered.

Above right: A monk's cell looking out over the Indian plains.

In fact he realized that he had been in a better state of mind when he was a child, sitting in the shade of a tree, than after all this self-torture. So, very disappointed with the failure of all this effort to find the truth and peace, Gautama decided to take some food and try some other way. *Legend* has it that Sujata, a milkmaid, offered him a bowl of rice and milk and that his five friends left him in disgust! Once he had got back some strength he walked to Gaya, in the modern Indian state of Bihar. There he decided that it was no good struggling to find *enlightenment*, he would just have to wait for it. So he sat down cross-legged under an Indian fig tree on a grass seat, and said to himself, 'Let my skin wither, my hands grow numb, my bones dissolve. Until I have gained understanding I will not rise from here'.

It took Gautama one night's *meditation* to achieve enlightenment. The word Buddhists use for enlightenment is 'Bodhi' and so Gautama became a 'Buddha', an 'Enlightened One'.

He had left home determined to discover the causes and cure of suffering. As dawn broke he believed that he had found them and in doing so had also found the secret of happiness.

During his long meditation Gautama was *tempted* to give up and go back to his life of pleasure as a prince in Kapilavattu. Buddhist *myths* say he was tempted by Mara, the god of *desire*, and his beautiful daughters. But, like Jesus in the story of the temptation by Satan in the desert, Gautama resisted.

One of the most important things Gautama realized that night was that anyone could find out what he had found out. They could do it by themselves, there was no need for priests or sacred books and there was no need to be rich. All that was needed was the courage to make up your own mind and change your own life. But he also realized that if he could tell others what he had found it would make it much easier for them.

'The Buddha, feeling *compassion* for the whole world, considered who among all living creatures, deserved first to hear the Law, the Dhamma. He remembered the five holy men with whom he had lived. Looking back for a moment at the Bodhi tree he set his feet upon the road, and in the deer park at Sarnath he came upon them.'

THE MIDDLE WAY

It was at Sarnath that Buddha first spoke about his discoveries to others and began the life of teaching which he was to follow until his death. Drawing a wheel in the air he showed that life and death are joined by rebirth, that nothing lasts for ever and that everything changes. This is why the Buddhist *symbol* is a wheel. The wheel has eight spokes because in his first *sermon*, the Sermon of the Turning of the Wheel of the Law, Buddha taught his new law, which has eight parts to it. This is the 'Eight-fold Path'. It is also called the 'Middle Way'. This is because it advises people to search for the truth by living carefully and *moderately* and to keep away from, on the one hand, luxury and, on the other hand, deliberate suffering and self-torture.

A gigantic statue from Ceylon. It is trying to express the *serenity* which came over Gautama as he gained Enlightenment.

Far right:
This is a painting from the Ajanta caves in India, an early Buddhist monastic community. It shows Mara's assault on Gautama, trying to frighten or tempt him away from his search for truth and peace.

Things to do

1. Find out what the words in italics mean in Chapter 3.
2. Imagine you are Gautama. Describe your wandering in search of a teacher and your life with the five holy men *or* draw a picture of Gautama when he was starving himself.
3. Why is the tree Gautama sat under called the 'Bodhi' tree?
4. Why is Buddha's teaching called the 'Middle Way'? How did he learn to avoid the extremes of luxury and asceticism? (You will need to sort out what some of these words mean first.)
5. Why is a wheel a good symbol for Buddha's ideas about birth, life and death?
6. If you have to decide something why is it sometimes hard to make up your own mind? Why do you sometimes need to be brave to do this?
7. Should you always be allowed to decide things for yourself? Make two lists, one showing the things that you should be allowed to decide about and the other listing the things which other people should decide for you. You could make drawings to illustrate your lists instead of writing them, if your prefer.
8. Buddhist stories say Gautama was tempted by Mara, the god of desire, to give up his efforts. How else can his temptation be explained?

A carving of Buddha riding an elephant, from the Ajanta caves.

4 Buddha's Life as a Teacher

FOLLOWERS Buddha devoted the rest of his life to spreading his teachings. Buddhists believe he did this simply because he wanted to help people, not because he felt superior to them or because he wanted to be a famous, powerful leader. Like Jesus, he converted many who became *disciples* and sent them out to *preach*. Also like Jesus, he travelled about his home country, teaching and helping anyone who would listen and relying on his followers and others to provide him and his closest disciples with food and shelter.

This is what he said to his disciples before he sent them out to teach, 'Go out for the benefit of the many and in compassion for the world. Point out the way to those who tread their path in darkness. Like the evening star give light and comfort to the toiling *pilgrim*. Find those who know even less than you do, those who are starving for the food of Truth. Let them hear the Law.'

Buddha went back to Kapilavattu and converted his father, his wife and son. Rahula became almost as important an assistant to him as his faithful attendant Ananda. Everywhere he went Buddha insisted that he only wanted to help others to escape from suffering. He talked about all sorts of things with the many types of holy men that he met on his travels: whether the universe was *eternal* or not; whether there is a life after death, etc. But Buddha himself returned to his own main concern over and over again: 'This, monks, I have declared: what is suffering, what is the cause of it, what is the cure of it and what is the Way to cure it.'

HIS TEACHING STYLE Buddha said that the wise man, 'Does not get involved in arguments . . . does not worry how the world began'. He often refused to answer questions about things which he thought were impossible to answer anyway. Other teachers of his time spent most of their lives thinking about the really mysterious things in life. Buddha thought that was a waste of time. This was because his was a very *practical* message, he just wanted to help people and thought that arguing and *speculating* did not help anyone.

To get over his ideas he would often tell stories, just as Jesus told parables. He pointed out that if a man was shot by an arrow he would not stop to ask lots of questions about the

Buddha teaching his followers (the little figures at the base of the statue). Note the halo again, and the guardian spirits.

person who fired it, whether he or she was short or tall, bald or hairy, married or unmarried, etc. All he would want to do was get the arrow out and stop the pain.

There is another famous story Buddha told to show how foolish and wasteful of time it was to quarrel and argue:

'Once upon a time a ruler of a city got so fed up with his councillors arguing and squabbling among themselves that he called them all into the great courtyard of the palace. He then had an elephant brought into the courtyard, followed by some blind beggars from the streets outside. He then asked the beggars to tell him what they thought the animal was. One blind man put his hand on the elephant's head and said it was a huge pot. Another put his hand on an ear and said it was a big fan. A third put his hand on one of the elephant's legs and said he was touching a tree. Another blind man caught hold of the trunk and shouted that there was a huge snake attacking him. The fifth felt the tuft on the elephant's tail and swore the animal was a broom. Then they all began quarrelling fiercely, each one certain he was right and the others were wrong. The ruler turned to his councillors and told them they were just like the blind men because they argued instead of listening to each other, they did not agree on anything and did not suggest anything which could help him rule his kingdom.'

Buddha also meant to say, through this parable, that there are many sides to the truth, many ways of looking at it, and it is a waste of time fighting over which way is the best one. It is far better to go out and do something to find the truth rather than waste your life discussing it.

Here is another parable. Buddha is trying to show his friend Yamalka that a person's *physical appearance* is not what that person really is.

'Suppose there is a householder or his son, rich and prosperous, and he has a body-guard and some man came along wanting to steal from and kill the wealthy man. The thief would think, "This householder is rich and he has a bodyguard. It will not be easy to take his life." He might approach the wealthy man and ask to be made his servant. Being appointed he would get up before his master, go to bed after him, notice what he wanted done, be well-behaved and polite. The householder would trust him. But when the man thought the householder trusted him, once he was alone with him he would take his life with a sharp sword.'
'What do you think, Yamalka, when the man asked to be taken on as a servant, even then he is a murderer, though the householder does not know it?'
'Yes, friend.'
'In the same way the ordinary person looks on his body and trusts it, thinking it is his *self*.

The early Buddhist
'Vihara' at Ajanta in
India, as it is today.
The natural caves
have been enlarged
and made into
monks' *cells* and into
shrines. Also there
are many carvings
and paintings
depicting Buddhist
beliefs and stories.

A colossal statue in
Ceylon depicting the
death of Buddha. The
faithful Ananda
stands by.

We know Buddha was a very good and popular teacher because Buddhism spread quickly all over India and soon became the main religion in other Asian countries, such as China and Japan. Buddha converted and sent out as preachers hundreds of *monks* ('Bhikkus'). He set up monasteries ('Viharas') as resting places for the monks during the monsoon season when travelling was hard. He also allowed an order of *nuns* to be established, though he seems to have been a bit unsure about this at first! Ananda, and his Aunt Gotami persuaded him.

Buddhists believe Buddha showed his *love* for *humanity* by not keeping his knowledge to himself but by going and working very hard, for many years, so as to teach it directly to as many people as possible. But in the end old age caught up with him:

'After many months and seasons had passed and when Buddha was in his eightieth year, during the course of a rainy monsoon he became ill. It was after he had eaten some mushrooms. Sharp pains entered his stomach, so much so that he was expecting death. He made up his mind that by an effort of will he would survive long enough to speak once more to his disciples before taking leave of them for ever.

The 'Great Stupa' at the ancient Buddhist centre of Sanchi in India.

'Ananda came to him and Buddha said, "O Ananda, now I am old and my journey is near its end. My body is like a worn-out cart held together only by the help of leather straps. Come then, let us go to the sala grove of the Malla Kings at Kushinara."
'So the Buddha, with a great many followers, went to Kushinara, a tiny, remote village near the Himalayas. In the sala grove Ananda made a bed for him, with its head to the north, towards the holy mountains. Then the Buddha spoke his last words, "My brothers, everything passes away, work hard to find your own salvation".'

The body of Gautama, the Buddha, was burnt on a funeral pyre of sweet, sandalwood logs and perfumed oils. His ashes were distributed among the kings of the places where he had lived and these kings built eight memorial buildings ('Stupas') for the *relics*. These became *shrines* for the followers of Buddha, together with his birth-place, Gaya, Sarnath and the site of his death at Kushinara.

Things to do

1. Find out the meaning of the words in italics in Chapter 4.
2. Why did Buddha need disciples?
3. Why did he use stories in his teaching?
4. What does his story about the man wounded by an arrow mean?
5. In the story of the elephant and the blind men which ruler is Buddha probably thinking of?
6. Tell the story of the elephant and the blind men from the point of view of one of the councillors or make a comic strip of the story.
7. What does it mean that there are many sides to the truth, or many ways of looking at it? Give some examples, from religion if you can.
8. In the story of the rich householder and the evil servant what does Buddha mean by saying that the servant is a murderer even when he has just been employed, long before he kills his master?
9. What do you think Buddha means by the word 'self' in this story.
10. Why was travelling hard during the Indian monsoon in Buddha's time?
11. What do Buddha's last words mean to you?

5 Buddha's Teachings

Not all religions have a 'founder'. Hinduism is the main religion of India today. It is many thousands of years old and, although the names of many great leaders of Hinduism are known, no one knows who began it or who wrote many of its sacred *scriptures*.

Buddha's teachings are based on the Hindu religion in which he was brought up, in just the same way as the teachings of Jesus arise from the Jewish religion of his parents and fellow Jews.

THE SERMON OF THE TURNING OF THE WHEEL OF THE LAW We have heard of this sermon before. In it Gautama explained what had been *revealed* to him at his enlightenment. After explaining the 'Middle Way' he went on to describe what he had discovered.

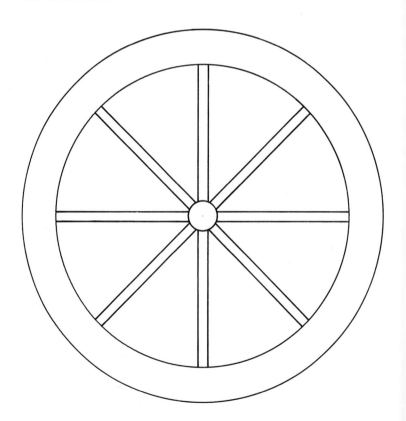

This wheel represents Buddha's teaching. The circle, the rim of the wheel, represents the cycle of birth, death and rebirth. The spokes stand for the eight-fold path.

1. *Life is suffering.* By this Buddha meant that life is full of unhappiness and disappointment because nothing lasts. Even if we get what we want we soon lose it again or we grow bored and dissatisfied with it. Most of us cannot even sit still for five minutes without beginning to feel a bit uncomfortable.

2. *Suffering comes from desire.* Because we are always wanting (*craving*) many different things, we suffer *frustration* and sadness when we cannot have these things, or lose them. It has been said that we love what we cannot have and hate what we cannot avoid. In particular we love life and hate death, we want health and fear sickness, we want safety and dislike danger. Because we cannot have these things that we want, at least not all the time, and because we have to face the things which we hate and fear, we suffer.

3. *Get rid of desire and you get rid of suffering.* If we can *extinguish* our desires, like putting out a flame, then suffering will vanish too. And evil will vanish also, because the worst aspects of human behaviour, like greed and hate, come from people wanting things which they cannot have.

4. *There is a way to blow out the flame of desire.* The way to get rid of desire and suffering is to follow the 'Eight-fold Path', which is also the 'Middle Way'.

This is a plan, like a training programme for a marathon runner. It starts quite easily and gets harder and harder.

There are eight steps on the way. First you must have *faith* in the Buddha's teaching. You need to *believe* that he followed the plan and ran the race and won! These are the first two steps.

Next you must learn to live properly, so the third to fifth steps are about *morality*. The last three steps are about meditation (which is important in Buddhism but which occurs in all religions).

1. *Right understanding.* Believe in the 'Four Noble Truths'.

2. *Right thoughts and intentions* . Do not live as if you were the most important person in the world. Think about other people first. Make sure your *motives* are no longer selfish.

3. *Right speech.* Stop telling lies, stop gossiping about others behind their backs, do not be rude or harsh when you talk to people.

4. *Right action.* Behave in a peaceful, kind and honest way, neither harming nor killing anything.

5. *Right livelihood.* Everyone should work hard at what they do best, but for the benefit of others and not just of themselves.

6. *Right effort.* Up to this point the training programme has allowed the follower of the 'Middle Way' to live a normal life and train at the same time. But once you have learnt to live by the guidelines laid down in the first five parts of the Eight-fold Path then you have to take the drastic step of concentrating all your efforts on the last three stages, if you want to get any further.

This means devoting your whole life to following the Buddha's Way, just as athletes in training for a world record, must spend all their time and energy preparing for the race.

7. *Right mindfulness.* Meditation is a way of *concentrating* your mind so as to know things which ordinary thinking cannot discover. 'Mindfulness' is a sort of meditation. Wherever you go, whatever you do, you must think for yourself, let no one else make up your mind for you. Also (and this is harder), you must 'watch yourself': be aware of what you are thinking and feeling and doing all the time, in other words be 'mindful' of yourself. While you are observing what you are doing you should try and remain *detached*, in a calm frame of mind, as if you were watching someone else.

8. *Right concentration.* This means meditating correctly. Gautama was able to work out how to do this on his own. Everyone else needs a 'Guru', or teacher. At this stage a Buddhist has the same experience that Buddha had beneath the Bodhi tree at Gaya. They have reached **Nirvana**, which is a new way of seeing the world. You are at peace because you are no longer troubled by desire. You are free because you are no longer 'a slave to desire'.

Things to do	1. Write out with care the Four Noble Truths and the Eight-fold Path. Write a sentence or two on each saying what they mean.
	2. Draw the symbol of Buddhism and label it with the parts of the Eight-fold Path.
	3. Write down or draw pictures of two things which most of us would like to have but which no one can have and two things which most of us do not want but which we all have to face.
	4. Write out a *graded* list of disappointments.
	5. We all have some sort of talent (we are all quite good at something). How could you put your talents to use, helping others?
	6. Make a list of the most powerful desires most of us have.
	7. Is it ever possible to get what you want and keep it?
	8. Make sure you have found out the meaning of each italicized word in the first part of Chapter 5.
	9. Write an essay or make a comic strip which begins with the words, 'I wish . . .'
	10. Try 'mindfulness' now, for a short while.

Nirvana means 'to blow out'. The person who completes the Eight-fold Path 'blows out' desire. But there are some strange side-effects! Buddha taught that when desire vanishes so does your 'self'. Perhaps this is best explained by thinking about two words: 'selfish' and 'selfless'. Selfish means wanting things for yourself. Selfless means being completely unselfish. Buddha teaches us that we are all selfish and this makes everyone's life less happy than it could be. But enlightened people are 'selfless', they are no longer *self-important* or *self-centred*, because they no longer feel the need to be selfish. They are no longer selfish because they have 'blown out' desire and experienced Nirvana.

Most people never sit down and think about who or what they really are. But this is what the Eight-fold Path is all about. And Buddha taught that once you have finished the path you realize that 'you', your *individuality*, your 'self', are no different from everything else because, like everything else, you, too, change and decay.

Are you the same person you were five or ten years ago? Did you exist in any way long before you were born? Are you exactly the same person now as you were ten minutes ago? Will the 'you' you are now be the same 'you' in sixty years' time? Buddhists talk about the 'self' or *personality* being *unreal*. It is unreal, they say, because it is as changeable and *impermanent* as the weather.

Nirvana is the 'blowing out' – the extinguishing – of all desire.

The head of the Buddha (from Thailand). This famous work of art tries to show the real peace and joy that Buddha achieved. Does it succeed in doing this?

So when you 'blow out' desire you 'blow out' your 'self' too. This sounds worrying to us, like a sort of death. But Buddha did not lose his individuality or '*character*' at Gaya, far from it, and Buddhists are very cheerful people. Their religion makes them calm and happy, on the whole. They believe that what is blown out is not real anyway, it is an *illusion*. It is an illusion to think that there is an unchanging 'I' at the centre of 'my' life. And this illusion is what causes desire and so it causes human suffering. So seeing the truth about it is something to look forward to!

Buddha always avoided discussing Nirvana because it is not an idea, or an object, but a state of mind which has to be experienced. In the same way that a marathon runner cannot put into words exactly how he felt during the last few miles of the race, so a Buddha cannot describe Nirvana in words. Like the marathon runner he says that, to find out, you must try it yourself. All Buddha would say was what Nirvana was not:

> 'Neither earth, nor water, nor fire, nor mind, nor *infinity*, nor nothing, nor *consciousness*, nor *unconsciousness*, nor this world, nor the next world, neither coming, nor going, nor staying, nor passing away, unborn, unmade, the end of pain.'

Here is a famous and popular Buddhist story, the 'Tale of the Five Pilgrims'. Remember that Gautama liked to use stories to illustrate his teachings. Like Jesus he knew that a story makes people listen and think far more successfully than a lecture! That is why this, and others, of his stories are sometimes called parables, which are teaching stories with a hidden moral, or spiritual, meaning. By making the meaning hidden Gautama (and Jesus) makes the listener interested, curious and ready to search out the meaning for themselves.

This tale is Buddha's way of showing how each person finds his or her own, personal, way to Nirvana.

> 'There was once a wise old *saint*. He had five disciples. When he was dying he said to them, "I have one last wish. When I am dead I want you all to make a pilgrimage to my home city, and there to pray for me and honour me". Although this city was a long way away the five disciples agreed immediately. Soon after the old man died.
>
> One morning they set off together down a long, dusty road, lined with trees, which pointed straight out across the hot plains of northern India. As they trudged along one of them got impatient: "I can't be bothered to dawdle along like this", he shouted, "I want to get there quickly and then get on with other things!" So he quickened his pace and very soon left them far behind. Week after week he pressed on, only stopping briefly at night for sleep, food and drink. Within a month he had reached his goal.
>
> Meanwhile another of the pilgrims was finding the going too fast for him. "I'm puffed out" he said to his friends. "Leave me here for a bit, I'll catch up" and he sat down under a tree and fell asleep. When he awoke he was all alone, so he walked a few miles to the next village and had a good meal and another sleep. Next day, feeling stronger he dawdled another few miles. In the end it took him almost a year to wander along the same road it had taken the first pilgrim one month to cover!

The remaining trio walked on cheerfully for a while together. But soon one of them began to worry, "Suppose we are on the wrong road? I don't know if my friends are sure of the right road anyway, and I am certainly not sure!" he muttered to himself. So he asked a farm worker digging by the road which was the safest and surest way to the city. "You must go to the left here", he was told, "Then straight on to the town and ask again". So this doubtful pilgrim said goodbye to his companions and set off on his own route. Every person he met he asked for directions. Every person gave him different ones. Eventually, after having walked backwards and forwards, up and down and round and round, over most of northern India he came to the city. It had taken him over two years to do it though!

Only two were left together after the doubtful pilgrim turned off the road. Unfortunately these two disliked each other. One of them had only become a follower of the saint because he hoped to make a lot of money by having followers of his own, who would pay him to teach them. But the old saint had died before he had learnt anything. Now he was fed up, with sore feet, little food, no money and a long, boring journey ahead. So he said to his fellow traveller, "I'm off home" and turned round and hitched a lift back. He soon forgot his promise, and tried to make a living from gambling. When this didn't work he took to stealing and ended up in prison. While inside he learnt new tricks of the thief's trade but because he was not very good at learning anything he was usually caught again, soon after being released. Many, many years went by. He began drinking heavily and taking various drugs. A doctor in prison warned him that because of this he would probably die very soon. When he heard this the reluctant pilgrim suddenly remembered his promise to the saint. Upon his release he set out for the city. Thirty years after he had first set out he finally arrived where he had promised (but originally not really wanted) to go.

The last pilgrim walked steadily on alone. One day he met a man bowed down beneath a heavy burden of wood. The pilgrim offered to share the load, and went with him to his house, many days walk from the road. The house was in a village of very poor people, who had to do the worst jobs for the rich landowners who lived on big farms. The pilgrim felt he could not leave, not until he had done what he could to help the villagers in their work, and in their struggles with the farmers. Then he returned to the journey, but almost every day he came across someone who needed a bit of help, or a bit of advice. Sometimes it wasn't a human but an animal which required his aid! In this way his journey became longer and slower. But he did reach the city in the end, after ten years travelling and working.'

Buddha used to tell this story to his disciples. Then he would set them arguing by asking, 'Which was the best pilgrim?' After a while Buddha would interrupt and say, 'Listen, you are missing the point: everyone is different. We are all like the five pilgrims. No one is a better or worse pilgrim on the journey towards Nirvana. We all have our own ways of travelling through life. The real question is which of these pilgrims are you like? Also, will you reach the goal in the end, as they all did in this life, or will you reach it in one of your future lives? For all people reach Nirvana in the end.'

'KARMA' AND 'REINCARNATION'

Two of the ideas Gautama learnt from the Saddhus whom he met before his enlightenment were 'karma' and 'reincarnation'. But Gautama adapted them to his own purpose and outlook.

When Gautama first realized that change and death were *universal* and *inevitable* he vowed to find a way out of the trap. The way out was the Eight-fold Path because, once the path is being followed and especially once Nirvana is reached, no more karma is being made. Karma, in Buddhism, means

A young Buddhist monk with his begging bowl.

43

selfish acts and feelings which lead us to being reincarnated or reborn, over and over again. 'Beings pass away and are reborn according to their karma', Buddha said.

He spoke of all the little things to which people become *attached*, which lead them to be reborn, 'Children and wife, slaves, goats, chicken, pigs, elephants, houses, cattle, gold.' Buddha meant that if you desire everything in life and life itself, then your burden of karma will go on growing and you will remain tied to the wheel of birth and death. In fact Buddhists believe that, for most of us, rebirth, many thousands of times, is inevitable. But, if you can stop desiring anything (including life itself) and if you can stop acting selfishly (with desire) then you will escape from rebirth (and suffering too, because of the first Noble Truth). You will then pass into Nirvana for ever. And the only road to this sort of 'heaven' is the Eight-fold Path.

Buddhists believe Gautama passed into Nirvana for ever at his death. He began his *quest* by experiencing a *revulsion* against the change, decay and suffering in life, on the streets of Kapilavattu. When he began teaching he would always try to make those who came to him for help face up to the fact that life could never be the way they wanted it to be. Then they too would come to the beginning of the path which the Buddha himself had trodden from Kapilavattu.

Once a young mother came to Buddha. In her arms was her small baby, which had just died. She was terribly upset and, like most people in her situation, was asking everyone, 'Why me?' She begged Buddha to help bring her baby back to life and to explain why such a thing had happened to her. Gautama told her to go into the nearby town and bring back a mustard seed from any house in which no similar disaster had happened. After some time she came back but without any seeds.

'My poor little son!' she cried. 'I thought you were the only one taken by death and that I was the only one to suffer this great sorrow. But now I see that everyone must bear it.'

Gautama said to her, 'Now you know the law for all things — that nothing lasts. Rich and poor must die. We are born with nothing and we will die with nothing. There is only one thing which can protect us and that is knowledge. Seek this and you will be free from death and sorrow.'

From that moment she was calm and became a follower of the Middle Way.

Things to do

1. Make a list of things which describe who you are and what you are like.
2. Do the same for a friend.
3. Compare lists.
4. Draw a comic strip or a diagram or a picture which *illustrates* the idea that everything changes.
5. Write down two reasons why the Buddhist symbol of a wheel with eight spokes, is a good one.
6. Make a twentieth-century version of the Buddha's list of things to which people get 'attached'.
7. Write a story or make a comic strip up about the lives you might have lived in the past or the lives you might live in the future (you will need to use your imagination here).
8. Prove *you* exist.
9. Is there any *evidence* for reincarnation?
10. Write out the meaning of words in italics in the second part of Chapter 5.
11. The story of the woman and her dead son is a 'teaching story'. What is it trying to teach?
12. What *exactly* does Buddha mean when he says to the sorrowing mother, 'Nothing lasts'?
13. Also, what sort of knowledge (or wisdom) does he mean she should try and acquire?
14. Similar stories are told of Jesus (see, for instance, Luke Chapter 7 verses 11 to 17 and Chapter 8 verses 40 to 56). But what is the main difference between the Christian and Buddhist stories? And what does this tell you about Jesus and Buddha and how they are regarded by their followers today?
15. What does the city stand for in the story of the 'Five Pilgrims'? Also, what is the meaning in the story of the five different journeys?
16. Is Buddha trying to make us choose and copy the best disciple? (Which one do you think is the best?)
17. This version of the story is much shorter than the original: *imagine* you were one of the pilgrims. Write, or make a comic strip, about your journey, or, draw a map, showing the five different journeys.

Thai Buddhist monks
at prayer.

Because Buddha said you did not need a priest (a Brahmin) or
the priest's holy book (the Vedas) to solve your problems he
became unpopular with the *authorities* of the places he
worked in. What is more he allowed anyone, of any caste, to
follow him, and he mixed freely with them. This made him
ritually unclean to a good Aryan, but it made him popular
with the poor and the outcasts of his society. Jesus did the
same thing with the outcasts of Palestine and had similar
problems with the religious leaders of his time.

Buddha used to say that a true Brahmin was not someone
who had simply been born into the right family, but someone
who had done something to deserve the honour. 'He who says
"bho" (a rude way of speaking to someone), a man of
possessions, is the Brahmin by birth. He who has nothing and
who wants nothing, I call a Brahmin.'

Buddha also said that the person 'who slays not, nor causes
to be slain, I call a Brahmin.' The Brahmins' religion had, as its
basic *ritual*, animal sacrifice on a large scale. Buddha
criticized this as being cruel and useless, and taught that only
'a sacrifice free from violence' was any good. By that he meant
charity, or 'alms-giving'. Buddha's insistence on non-violence
('Ahimsa') to all creatures is one of the main characteristics of
Buddhism today and is why Buddhists tend to be *vegetarians*.

This word means 'Assembly' and applies to all followers of
Buddha, especially monks and nuns, who practise and pass on
the Dhamma, (the 'Teachings' or the 'Truth'). During his life
Buddha, with the help of friends, worked out a set of rules for
Buddhist 'lay-people' (ordinary followers), monks and nuns,
which have hardly changed since his time.

We know that Buddha spent a lot of time talking to his 'lay'
followers about how to go on living an ordinary life and at the
same time follow the Eight-fold Path. To help them to do this
he laid down the 'Five Precepts' which all Buddhists are
expected to keep:

Do not kill.
Do not steal.
Do not take part in sexual misconduct.
Do not lie.
Do not drink alcohol or take drugs.

The monks, devoting their entire life to the Middle Way,
were allowed only the simplest possessions, a robe or two, a
begging bowl, and possibly also a razor and a *rosary*. They had
to keep the Five Precepts and five more too:

Do not eat after midday.
Do not join in singing and dancing.
Do not use cosmetics or wear jewellery.
Do not have a high, soft bed.
Do not accept money, only food, from people.

Buddhist monasteries are still run in accordance with these rules.

There are eight additional rules for nuns, which seem to have been designed to make sure that the nuns and monks did not distract each other and also to make sure that the monks had some control over the nuns! Nevertheless when Gotami, Buddha's aunt, was asked if she still wanted to become a nun despite these extra rules she said, 'Just as a woman who is young and fond of adornment, after washing her head, is given a garland of lotus or jasmin, or rosewood flowers, takes it with both hands and puts it on her head, so do I take on myself these eight strict rules.'

Things to do

1. Find out the meaning of the words in italics in the third part of Chapter 5.
2. What does Buddha think a real Brahmin is like?
3. The Israelite prophet Isaiah lived in about the same time as Buddha. Find out what Isaiah says in the Book of Isaiah, Chapter 1, verses 10–16, in the Old Testament. Did Buddha say anything similar? Who to?
4. Is charity a sort of sacrifice? What sort?
5. Is killing animals for food cruel? Could you give up meat?
6. If people like eating meat so much why do we not eat human meat too?
7. Copy the ten rules for monks.
8. What is the purpose of such rules?
9. Imagine you are marooned on an island with a group of other people. Would you have a leader? How would you choose one if you did? Make a list of rules to help you all survive and get on with each other.
10. Many Buddhists are Pacifists because of Buddha's teachings on non-violence. What is Pacifism? Is it always right to be a Pacifist or is it always wrong?
11. Would you ever need courage to be a Pacifist? If your answer is 'Yes' say when. If 'No' explain why.

The account of Gautama's relationship with his followers is not complete without mentioning the revolt which took place against him, led by his cousin Devadatta.

Devadatta had been envious of Gautama when they had both lived together in the palace at Kapilavattu, probably because Gautama was so much the king's favourite. It is also suggested that he was, briefly, a rival for Yasodhara. But when Gautama came back to his home to preach and convert, after his enlightenment, Devadatta was one of those who became a close follower and believer.

For many years all went well: Gautama's young cousin helped to organize the growing monastic order and there was no sign of his earlier dislike for his now famous relative. This situation changed when members of other religious groups, who were competing with the Buddhists for new followers, began to scorn 'The Sons of the Sakya' (Gautama and his monks) for leading a too comfortable life. These enemies of Buddha criticized him for allowing his monks to sleep in a bed, wear simple but tidy and clean clothes and consume reasonable amounts of food and drink. Clearly they believed that only the most harsh and restricted way of life was suitable for a truly religious person. We have already seen that Gautama rejected these ideas when he left the Saddhus and their ascetic practices behind, before his enlightenment.

So this criticism should have been no problem to him, except that suddenly members of his own order began to say similar things and they were led by Devadatta. This small group of *dissenters*, insisted that, basically, Gautama was too 'soft' on his followers. The Five Precepts were not strict enough. To them should be added 'Five Practices'. These stated that all the monks should live alone, well away from villages and towns. They should never accept any invitations from ordinary people but should live entirely on the very simplest of food, which they should only get by begging. They should wear rags, and never clothes which had been given to them and they should also never even enter a house.

Gautama opposed these suggestions. We know that his own experience taught him that such harsh discipline did not bring peace and wisdom. He was also worried that they would be too much of a burden to impose on all his followers. Gautama was always *tolerant* of the differences between various human beings; for some the strict rules urged by Devadatta would be fine; for many others they would be impossible and this would

Indian Temple sculptures of Hindu gods and the Hindu heaven. Most people in Buddha's time worshipped similar gods. Buddha seems to have had very little to say about whether such beings really existed. You should understand though that Hindu ideas about their *deities* are very different from the beliefs the Greeks had about their gods and goddesses.

prevent them even starting on the long road towards Nirvana. For Buddha, this was the main reason to argue against the *puritans* in his monastic community. After all, he was concerned to help everyone and not just the few who found the sacrifices required by the '*calling*' of religion easy. Most of his followers found the Five Precepts difficult and even beginning the Eight-fold Path a great struggle!

Devadatta lost the argument. Buddhist literature shows that he did not accept this. He was a 'bad loser' and all his old envy and dislike of his cousin came out again. He was particularly friendly with a local chieftain or king. From him he borrowed some soldiers to kill Gautama. They waited with drawn swords behind a big wooden door for Buddha to pass by. But as they sprang out at him he spoke to them and his calmness and courage shamed them, so that instead of killing him they became followers. (Jesus had a similar effect sometimes on people who should have been his enemies. See, for instance, Luke Chapter 23, verses 47 to 48). Devadatta also tried, unsuccessfully, to kill Gautama by rolling a large rock down on him as he walked below.

The most famous incident concerns the elephant Nalagiri. Buddha was visiting the town where this animal was kept. Devadatta knew that, besides being a very fine and famous *ceremonial elephant*, Nalagiri had a fierce and *unpredictable* temper. He persuaded the elephant's keepers to mix strong alcohol in with his food and then release him into the town while Gautama was out begging. The huge animal charged down the narrow street, smashing down shops and market stalls, crushing people. Everyone ran, except Buddha who stood, calm and unafraid. Nalagiri came to a halt, knelt down and obediently allowed himself to be led away. For a devout Buddhist this story illustrates Devadatta's evil and Buddha's power. For non-Buddhists it may seem incredible, but remember, the important thing in many religious stories is their meaning, not their details. Also, some people do seem to have great, natural, influence over animals. Soon after this Devadatta died, his life a total failure. Nevertheless, some Buddhist books depict Buddha prophesying that his enemy would, in a future life, reach Nirvana. This does not just show Buddha as forgiving; it also shows how Buddhists believe that anyone can reach Nirvana and that everyone WILL, eventually. (What other Buddhist story you have read has a similar meaning?)

For Buddhists today Devadatta is more important as a symbol than as a person. He stands for the dangerous desires which we all have, dangerous because they disturb us and prevent us from completing the Eight-fold Path. Dangerous also because they can become so powerful that they rule our lives. These desires, which Devadatta displayed so clearly, are envy, ambition and greed.

The story of the disagreement between Devadatta and Gautama is the story of a *schism*. This is a common occurrence in religion; when disagreements between people lead to the development of separate branches or 'schools' within a religion. A famous example is the schism known as the Reformation, which began with one man, Martin Luther, deciding that certain things were wrong in his religion (Christianity) in his time. This led to the great division we now have between Roman Catholics and Protestants ('protesters' meaning followers of Martin Luther). We will see later that various Buddhist 'schools' have evolved too.

An interesting comparison can be made between Devadatta and Judas Iscariot. Many Christian *scholars* today believe Judas betrayed Jesus because he was disappointed with him. He had hoped Jesus would lead the Jews against the Romans in an all-out war. When Jesus refused, Judas, like Devadatta, instead of giving up, acted violently. It is also possible that Judas envied Jesus' influence over others, in the same way as Devadatta envied Gautama. Maybe Judas thought the peaceful, calm Jesus was simply not 'firm' enough too. In the cases of Judas and Devadatta it is hard to say now what really drove them to do what they did. Was it *idealism* (did they really believe they were right and their leaders wrong?), or was it simply personal dislike, jealousy and ambition?

Things to do

1. Why is Devadatta still remembered by Buddhists, do you think?
2. Why do you think he rebelled against Buddha?
3. Is it possible for a leader to 'live up to the expectations' of *all* his or her followers? (Give reasons for your answer.)
4. What is a 'bad loser'? Are you one?
5. What does the Devadatta story tell us *about Gautama*?
6. What was Devadatta envious of and greedy for?
7. Buddhists would say that greed and envy are desires. Are they? They would also say they cause suffering. Do they? (Do not forget to *explain* your answers, whatever they are).
8. What is *ambition*? Is it good or bad or neither (or both!)?
9. Make a list of your ambitions. Try to illustrate your list.
10. Is there a difference between arguing and quarrelling? *Write* about this *or* make a comic strip.
11. Imagine you were Devadatta. Describe in *any way you can*, your feelings and your plans, *or* write a short play about the Devadatta story.
12. Go through the last part of Chapter 5 and work out what the words in italics mean. Write the meanings down.
13. Here are two further examples of disagreements within a religion (*not* between two different religions). Find out what you can about one, or both:
    (a) The religious situation in Britain before the civil war in the 17th century.
    (b) The problems Moses had with the Israelites during their wanderings in the desert. The Israelites, like Devadatta, seem to have at times been less than pleased with their leader! (You will find these stories in the Bible, in the Book of Exodus, especially Chapters 2 to 5; 14 to 17; 19 and 20; 32).

For reading and discussion

1. In Chapter 5 we have looked at Buddha's basic teachings. They are a bit odd, coming from someone who is said to have founded a religion. Compare Buddha with Jesus or Muhammad:

   Does he tell us how to get to heaven or avoid hell?
   Does he perform miracles?
   Does he mention God?
   Does he talk about the creation?
   Does he talk about the end of the world or of Judgement Day?

   Were his ideas *revealed* to him, or did he work them out himself?

2. Buddha does tell his followers about good and bad behaviour. But what is the reason for his rules on how to behave? Is it to avoid *sin* and so get to heaven? Does he talk about sin at all?

3. Buddha's friends and followers did not worship him as a god as, for instance, Jesus came to be regarded soon after his death. Only much later did Buddhism came to have gods and super-human beings like other religions.

4. Buddhism has been called an 'atheistic' religion. Why? It has also been said that it is not a religion at all but a 'way of life' or a 'philosophy'. Is it? (You will have to decide what a religion is first!)

The huge statue of
Buddha at Kamakura
in Japan. What
impression is it
trying to create?

6 How do we know about Buddha?

All Buddhists are expected to say a short prayer every day. It is called the 'Three Jewels'.

> I go for *refuge* to the Buddha.
> I go for refuge to the Dhamma.
> I go for refuge to the Sangha.

We have learnt something about the Buddha and the Sangha. The Dhamma is the 'Truth' or the 'Teachings'. It is also the title of the most important Buddhist sacred book.

THE SPOKEN AND WRITTEN WORD Gautama probably did not write his ideas down. It is possible that some of his friends did but as that would have happened about 2500 years ago we certainly do not have their notes now! But soon after Buddha died in 483 BCE the teachings would have been written down. Firstly, because those who had heard Buddha preach to them were getting old and younger people wanted a record of the teachings before the old disciples died. Secondly, because Buddhists began arguing among themselves about what Buddha had actually said and meant and about who was the rightful leader, now the Master was gone. Rival groups of Buddhists had the teachings collected and written down and then insisted that their version was the only right one and could never be changed.

But unfortunately even these early writings have vanished. What we have now are many, very old, works which are copies of copies of copies of original writings long since vanished. So how do we know if, where they state that Buddha said something, he actually did say it?

We cannot be absolutely certain but we can give a few reasons for accepting some Buddhist writings as being close to what Buddha said and meant:

1. Most Buddhists of different '*schools*' and countries, while disagreeing over many things, do agree about which are the oldest writings of their religion. And they all accept that these writings are as close to Buddha's own voice as it is possible to get.
2. In India, in the third century BCE, a great king, the Emperor Ashoka, became a Buddhist. He spread the Buddhist *doctrine* all over India and had many of the teachings carved on pillars or on rocky cliffs. These survived until now and from them we can tell that Buddhism in Ashoka's time,

which was close to the lifetime of the Buddha, was very similar to the Buddhism which we can read about in the oldest Buddhist *scriptures* we have today.

THE SACRED
BOOKS OF
BUDDHISM

Two thousand years ago there were many different Buddhist schools, just as there are different Christian *denominations*, agreeing over many things, arguing over others, today. There are not many Buddhist schools now but one of them has, as its sacred *literature*, what is accepted to be the oldest collection of teachings by Buddha and stories about him.

The school is called the 'Therevada', 'School of the Elders', and it is found mainly in Sri Lanka, Burma and Thailand. Its holy books are called the 'Pali Canon', which means the sacred writings in the Pali language. Many of the words for Buddhist ideas which we have used are in Pali. For instance, the Pali word for suffering, as in the first Noble Truth, is 'Dukkha'. As Buddha himself spoke a long-dead language called Magadhi, we can see that these books must be *translations*.

Bodhisattvas in a painting of a Buddhist heaven.

Statues of Buddha in the great Wat Po Temple in Bangkok. Thailand is still a strongly Buddhist nation.

The Pali Canon is divided into three parts or 'Pitakas', which means 'baskets'. So the three parts as a whole is called the 'Tripitaka'. The three parts are:

1. The Dhamma Pitaka. This contains the speeches or 'discourses' of Buddha, called in Pali the 'Suttas'. The Dhamma Pitaka is mainly Buddha's teachings.
2. The Vinaya Pitaka. This lists instructions for monks and nuns.
3. The Abhidhamma Pitaka. This contains more Suttas.

(We have a list of the Suttas in each Pitaka, from 247 BCE, which agrees with the contents of each, today.)

59

The main disagreement within the Buddhist community today is between the Hinayana and Mahayana 'Churches', just as in Christianity the most important division is between Roman Catholic and Protestant Churches. The words 'Hinayana' and 'Mahayana' mean 'Small Vehicle' and 'Great Vehicle', of the Buddhist message. As you might realize it was a follower of Mahayana who thought these titles up!

The Therevada school is a Hinayana *sect*. Zen Buddhism, in Japan, or Tibetan Buddhism, are Mahayana. Mahayana Buddhists assert that Hinayana does not know the whole of the Buddha's teaching and they claim that the sacred books which are exclusive to them contain much essential teaching, passed down directly from the Buddha. Most of these works are in Sanskrit and were certainly written down later than the Pali Canon, for instance, the Prajnaparamita, the 'Great Wisdom' literature. However, both Buddhist groups acknowledge the Pali Canon as being of basic and ancient importance. In the same way as Protestant and Roman Catholic Churches both use the Bible, but the Roman Catholic Bible has several more books in it than the Protestant one (see if you can find out about this).

The Mahayana teachings are very often more complicated and *mystical* than those of Hinayana Buddhism. It was Mahayana Buddhism in India, China and Tibet which made *deities* an important feature of this type of Buddhism. Despite Buddha's silence on the matter Mahayana Buddhists believe that there are many heavens (and hells). In these heavens 'Bodhisattvas' rule. These are beings who are ready for Nirvana, after many thousands of lives of preparation, but who are deliberately avoiding it in order to remain available to human beings who need help. Gautama himself was the greatest Bodhisattva, before his final life, according to these beliefs. Buddhists can pray to and meditate upon these divine beings in order to progress further along the path to enlightenment.

It is important to keep in mind the fact that within Mahayana itself there are many divisions. In Japan, for instance, there is one sect which is devoted to the Bodhisattva Amida. By repeating his name over and over they hope to be reborn in his heaven, 'The Pure Land'. From there it is only a short step to Nirvana! In the same small country Zen Buddhism concentrates entirely on meditation and mental and physical exercises, with hardly a mention of Bodhisattvas.

In the Pitakas there are, scattered about, small bits of *biography*. The people who wrote them seem to have been more concerned with what Buddha said than with what he did. The writers of the Gospels seem to have had the same attitude towards Jesus. Complete biographies of the life of Buddha were not written down until many hundreds of years after his life. Many of the stories about Buddha's life that we have read come from these later works.

All this means is that we can be more certain that the *sayings* of Buddha (in the Dhamma Pitaka) are likely to be correct than we can be that the *stories* from the later works are completely true. But, we have also read bits of *autobiography*, where Buddha himself describes things which he had done, for instance, when he left home, or when he starved himself. Many of these come from the oldest parts of the Pali Canon, as do the accounts of the first sermon and of the Buddha's death.

But the stories of his life as a prince, the stories of Sujata and Mara, and the stories of the events surrounding his birth all come from later works and we cannot be sure of them. In any case, for a Buddhist, the description of the very special baby born to Queen Maya is important because of what it means to him or her. It tells the Buddhist that, long ago, someone unique was born, who, because of all the work and suffering he had gone through in thousands of previous lives, was born to reach perfection and to reveal to anyone who wanted to listen the way to true peace and happiness.

This is a Buddhist prayer. It is written in the Pali language. It means, 'Honour to him, the Blessed One, the Worthy One, the Enlightened One'. The last Pali word has been enlarged. It means, 'The Enlightened One', in other words 'The Buddha'.

नमो तरस भगवतो

अरहतो सम्मासंबुद्धरस

सम्मासंबुद्धरस

A 200 foot statue of Buddha at Bamiyan in Afghanistan. This is now a predominantly Muslim country.

Things to do 1. Find out what the words in italics mean in Chapter 6.
  2. Make notes on the Pali Canon. State what it is; what is in it, etc. List all the important facts about it.
  3. Write an *autobiographical* account of a very important event in your life;
     or
  4. Write a *biography* of yourself, from someone else's point of view.
  5. Go back through this book and make a *dictionary* of Buddhist terms, with their meanings.
  6. Write the story of the Buddha's life as if you had known him *or* as if you were writing a newspaper article about him.
  7. Make a comic-strip version of the Buddha's life or draw a series of pictures showing the main events in his life.
  8. Copy this down carefully (except for the words in italics).

  The oldest Buddhist texts we have are in Pali. Later Buddhist literature was written in the ancient Indian language Sanskrit.
  Dhamma is a Pali word. It translates into Sanskrit as Dharma. Nirvana is the Sanskrit way of writing the Pali word Nibbana.
  The Pali name for what we call the Sermon of the Turning of the Wheel of the Law is the: Dhamma-cakka-ppavattana Sutta.
  The Pali name for the Sutta (in Sanskrit Sutra) which tells the story of the death of Buddha is the: Mahā Parinibbāna Sutta. (*What word is hidden in here*?)
  Words which have an 'a' in them which has a line on top (ā) are pronounced with a 'long a' sound (as in 'car' and 'bar').
  The Jātakas are an old collection of stories about Buddha's many lives. How is the word Jātaka pronounced? How is the word Tathāgata pronounced? (What does it mean? See Chapter 1 page 10.)